MW01119900

# THE OLD MAN'S GUIDE TO INVESTING

*A Silver Lining for Those Golden Years*

# *A DIFFERENT APPROACH FOR YOUR IRA AND YOUR 401(k) AND 403(b) ROLLOVERS*

By

## Larry A. McCue

Disclaimer: While the author was an employee of Edward D. Jones and Company, now known as Edward Jones, the company mentioned herein has had no input in this guide. The content herein is solely the opinion of the author and in no way reflects upon Edward Jones.

© 2010 Larry A. McCue
All Rights Reserved.

No part of this publication may be reproduced, stored in a retrieval system, or transmitted, in any form or by any means, electronic, mechanical, photocopying, recording, or otherwise, without the written permission of the author.

First published by Dog Ear Publishing
4010 W. 86th Street, Ste H
Indianapolis, IN 46268
www.dogearpublishing.net

ISBN: 978-160844-728-2

This book is printed on acid-free paper.

Printed in the United States of America

# Acknowledgements

Bringing this guide to print has become a family project. I would have been unable to complete this guide without the love and patience of my wife and three daughters, and in turn, their respective spouses.

Thanks to my wife, Sylvia, for her patience, support and help while we navigated the ins and outs of taking a book from blank sheets of paper to the end product. Getting the pages back and forth to the editor electronically was sometimes a challenge and thankfully she was able to help in that regard.

Thanks to Amy for editing the guide and helping to coordinate the publishing.

Thanks to Lisa for her typing skills and to Thad for his computer support.

Thanks to Jill for finding a book on self-publishing that proved to be very helpful, and to Todd for helping us come up with a book title.

Thanks also to Keith and to Mike for providing a fresh eye and offering their suggestions.

# Table of Contents

# INTRODUCTION

## THIS GUIDE WAS WRITTEN TO EMPOWER THE RETIREE OR SOON TO BE RETIREE

This guide was written because of an article that appeared in the July-August, 2004 AARP Bulletin entitled, "Tossing Good Money after Bad Advice." It was a discouraging article. I wanted to provide hope for retirees and those about to retire. I felt the need to demonstrate to retirees and to employees who have accumulated an asset base within their retirement accounts that it is possible for them to continue to grow their assets during retirement while still taking distributions. It can be done by investing in dividend-paying stocks within the retirement account while using "The Rule of 72" and the 10 year Treasury bond yield as benchmarks.

First, however, I needed to put my theory to the test. I began my retirement 14 years ago, refining my theory during the ensuing years. So far, it has worked well for me so it became time to put it into print.

Chapters 1 and 2 discuss the article and compare it with the results of my personal IRA rolled from a 401(k) after 14 years, from April of 1996 through March of 2010. The time period encompasses the "tech bubble" of 2000 through 2003 and the severe downturn of the stock market beginning in late 2007 and lasting through March of 2009. The study and analysis has helped develop guidelines for successful investing with an eye focused on the time at 70 ½ years old when one is required to take minimum distributions from their plan.

Make no mistake by assuming there will be no errors in investment decisions during your investment plan.

The stock market is like life itself. You need to expect the unexpected. Having said that, by setting goals and adhering to those goals, the stock market is your best protection on what I consider the biggest danger to retirees today, **inflation!** My plan details the mistakes made as well as the successes. Keep in mind that the most astute investor will make errors in judgment. The secret is to keep the errors at a minimum in order for you to withdraw enough cash from your plan to accomplish the projected goal set when you retire.

The best feature of this guide is that I am not trying to sell you anything. I sincerely believe that by reading this guide and understanding what you need to accomplish, your goal will allow you to relax the next time the stock market recedes.

# THE INSPIRATION
# FOR THIS GUIDE

This guide was written because of an article entitled, "Tossing Good Money After Bad Advice" in the July-August 2004, AARP Bulletin. The article's focus was on Proctor and Gamble employees in Augusta, Georgia. A broker had given a dinner meeting where he stated he could make anyone's retirement grow up to 20% a year using a strategy involving blue chip stock. One poor gentleman, then 50, had worked at a P&G detergent plant for more than 30 years and wasn't really ready to retire. But, he had suffered two heart attacks in the past, and thanks to the P&G employee-stock program, his nest egg had grown to $1.3 million. Think of it, here's a man who followed the rules of savings. Even with his health problems, he had managed to save $1.3 million over a lifetime. A broker from a national brokerage firm told him he "could make a bigger salary by retiring than by staying on the job." The sad scenario began in 1998 when the P&G employee rolled over his P&G account into an IRA. According to the article, the account sank lower and lower until it had lost about 1 million dollars. For a man with heart problems, I am surprised that he survived. He, along with other clients of this particular broker complained repeatedly. They were told it was merely a market correction. Then the broker, "who apparently didn't believe his own advice, began shifting client money into risky tech stocks, which only accelerated the plunge. Millions of dollars in assets held by dozens of P&G workers went down the drain." A footnote to this article was that in April, 2004, the Georgia Secretary of State announced a settlement with the brokerage firm that provided $27 million in restitution for 119 investors, about half of them P&G retirees. The brokerage firm called the Georgia case an isolated incident involving one branch. Of course, the individual involved no longer works for the firm. The P&G employee high-lighted by the article went back to work in late 2000 at the age of 56. He works as a warehouse supervisor earning about a third of what he made at P&G.

Additional examples of malfeasance by brokers appear in the same article. Employees of East Ohio Gas and Rub-bermaid were persuaded by brokers to accept buy-out offers and subsequently saw their nest eggs dwindle as the risky stocks they had been put into tanked. Arbitration panels ruled in favor of two of these employees with large awards from two different national brokerage firms.

My question is where was the due diligence that should have been in place?  Brokers are supposedly required to know their clients and the goals of their clients.  Where was the management that is supposed to judge a broker's performance and decide if he is following the parameters set out by the client?

The reader may be thinking, "I understand the problem, now give me your solution."  Although in my opinion, the brokerage firms responsible for the cases cited did a miserable job, a renegade broker can cause considerable damage before being identified. Therefore, you need to have a clear understanding of what you want your asset base to accomplish. Also, if you are using a broker for your investments, you need to listen and decide if you are comfortable with what he is saying. Any broker that promises you a 20% return on your assets is trying to 'snow' you. Walk away as fast as you can.

As you read the guide, keep in mind it is being written for the over 50 crowd that has an asset base in their retirement accounts, whether it is from a 401(*k*), a 403(*b*), or an individual retirement account (IRA). In any case, a vital condition is that the person has an asset base, and wants to use that base to grow as well as furnish income for his or her retirement.

The investment advice is nothing new. Back in the 1950's the common quote was that a conservative dividend-paying stock should be in the portfolio of a widow. Now our government has provided us with a law that allows our retirement accounts to be rolled over into an IRA upon retirement. Guess what! That keeps our asset base from being taxed and keeps the entire bank of assets in place. Of course, income tax will have to be paid when a withdrawal is made, but one can plan his withdrawals to minimize the tax consequence. Even better, if your IRA is willed to your spouse upon death, there is still no income tax until withdrawal. This means that all dividend income and capital gains in this pool are not taxed when acquired. One word of caution: When rolling over your 403(b) or 401(k) into your IRA, do not take direct possession of the assets. Roll the assets from one trustee to another trustee for your benefit. This keeps your assets free of income tax but still allows you to self-direct your investments.

One additional item should be mentioned. Our government has now provided us with one more way to avoid income tax when the Roth IRA was signed into law. Since the Roth IRA allows us to withdraw certain amounts from it without paying income tax, it could be used beneficially by certain tax payers. (You should check with a professional when funding your investment plans.) The difference is that you don't get to deduct your Roth IRA contribution as an expense when funding your retirement plan(s). I believe in the old adage "A bird in the hand is worth two in the bush." In other words, my belief is that those who are eligible for a retirement fund deduction should take full advantage of it before paying into a Roth IRA.

# AN ATTEMPT TO COMPARE APPLES TO APPLES

When you look at my Individual Retirement Account balance of $829,704 at 12-31-07, it is difficult to understand how the broker involved in the article entitled, "Tossing Good Money after Bad Advice," managed to lose a million dollars of a $1.3 million dollar asset base. Then I began examining the article closer and comparing the year end balances of my IRA with what the article indicated had happened. First, the man who the article documented retired in 1998, two years after I did. At December 31, 1998, (see EXHIBIT II) I had withdrawn cash from my IRA of $57,895, and my total fund balance of $587,324, was $123,481 more than the balance of $463,843 from December 31, 1996, the first year of my retirement. The article states that for the first two years everything went well. At the end of December 31, 2000, I had withdrawn $87,895 and my asset balance was $682,224, an increase of $218,381 from my starting balance of $463,843. I would say everything went well. But, after withdrawing another $47,000 during 2001 and 2002, my asset balance was $508,802 at the end of 2002, a decrease of $173,422 from the December 31, 2000, balance of $682,224. Here, I have to take an educated guess of what was happening between the broker and his client. The retiree states, "I must have asked him 10 times, 'Is my principle going to be safe?'" Remember what happened at the end of the decade? Tech stocks were advancing to unheard of P/E ratios.[1] Then, in 2001

[1] P stands for 'price of stock per share.' E stands for 'earnings of stock per share.' By dividing the earnings per share into the price per share, you arrive at the P/E ratio. If the stock price is extremely high in relation to the earnings per share, you have an extremely high P/E ratio. If the earnings per share is higher and you divide it into the same price, the P/E ratio is lower. Therefore, a lower P/E ratio signifies a safer stock price than a higher P/E ratio. To simplify even further, look at a business without stock. As an example, you invest $10,000 and earn $1,000 on your investment. You made 10% and your P/E ratio is 10. If you made $500 on your $10,000 investment, your P/E ratio would be 20, i.e., $500 divided into $10,000.

and 2002, the market corrected and it was painful for anyone holding tech stocks that had no dividend payouts. The article states the broker transferred out of "blue chip" stocks into risky tech stocks. The broker let the client color his judgment. In trying to please, the broker went after some fast gains and must have invested in tech stocks close to their highs immediately before the bubble broke. This is a lesson that should be learned in goal setting and sticking with the goal. The lesson to be learned is to buy dividend-paying stocks to cushion the downward spiral when it happens. The article I refer to appeared in the July-August, 2004, AARP Bulletin. This leads me to believe the account was taken back by the retiree sometime in 2003, before the asset balances had a chance to recuperate. Again, the December 31, 2007, balance of my IRA was $829,704 after withdrawing cash of $231,196, and beginning with an asset base of $463,841 eleven years ago. This performance teaches at least three things:

- First, dividends are important.
- Second, one should keep with the goal of holding good stocks with rising dividends.
- Third, do not sell when a market correction begins if the first two criteria are present.

While examining my IRA balances, I discovered a very important fact. Between December 31, 2005 and December 31, 2007, a period of two years, my asset balance increased $145,616 after withdrawing cash funds of $41,196. The increase appears to be overdone, and I can probably expect a retraction over the next one or two years. What should be done? (See EXHIBIT I.) Nothing, I can sleep at night. My individual stock fund holds $573,388 (representing 69.11% of my total fund) in basic industry stocks made up of electric, gas and telephone utilities, and gas and oil producing stocks. Most of these stocks have a history of rising dividends and at December 31, 2007, the basic industry stocks had paid dividends of $22,523 during 2007, a figure within approximately $10,000 of my 2008 minimum withdrawal figure. Total dividends paid during 2007 were $28,503. An additional $29,486 or 3.55% of the fund was in cash and 17.82% of the fund was invested in an international stock mutual fund. What I considered to be low risk assets total $750,735 or 90.48% of the total fund balance of $829,704. The two risky parts of the fund were financial services and health care representing 4.14% of the fund. In 2008, I added to those two sectors. Time will tell if I guessed correctly. The exciting fact of my examination is that if the utility stock prices contract as I expect, I can add another 2-3% in this sector with dividends averaging over 5%. This is while the ten year bond yield is presently below 4%, and the Federal Reserve Board is reducing short term interest every chance it gets, thereby lowering certificate of deposit and money market interest rates.

Since this chapter deals with the article "Tossing Good Money after Bad Advice," let us return to the $1.3 million asset base transferred to an IRA in 1998. The question to the retiree should have been, "How much money do you need to withdraw from your IRA yearly?" If he had replied $44,000 or less, the broker could have made a happy client. The investment: $100,000 in cash; $100,000 in one or two international stock mutual funds; $1,100,000 in basic industry type stocks such as electric, gas, and oil producing companies and maybe one or two consumer staple companies as long as the overall dividends are 4% of $1,100,000  or $44,000, slightly over the present 10 year Treasury bond yield. The dividends would have paid the cash withdrawals, and as the dividends grew, the broker could have added to the stocks with the help of the free $100,000 in cash that remained after the original investment. The client should have focused on available cash for investment and withdrawal and not on stock prices and fund growth. Over time the fund will grow without extreme risk. Keep in mind that, although you may feel richer, your IRA fund is an investment that will fluctuate in value.

# DISCUSSION OF MY
# IRA HISTORY

In the fall of 1995 I was going to reach the age of 59 in December. I wanted to retire while I could still enjoy quality time traveling with my wife. I calculated what my cash needs would be coming from my 401K plan if I rolled it into an IRA. I theorized that if I invested my cash into basic growth and income stocks, and had the dividends deposited from these stocks into my IRA money market, I could withdraw an average of $20,000 yearly, begin drawing social security at age 62, and still have my IRA fund grow. To accomplish these results, I needed to invest my 401(k) proceeds entirely into dividend-paying stocks, which was not what any investment advisor could recommend. Since I had other stock &

bond investments owned by my wife and me, I decided to take the plunge.

On May 10, 1996, I received $408,181 from my 401K plan which I rolled into my IRA. In addition, on December 31, 1996, I also held $40,733 in American Funds, Capital World Growth & Income Fund. This was a fund invested in large company international funds. Notice that this international stock exposure represented approximately 10% of my IRA. I believed that everyone should have some foreign stocks to provide diversification of assets. It was decided that the foreign investment should be invested through a stock mutual fund. The decision was made to keep this part of my IRA intact and let it build, if possible, until it reached a maximum value representing 20% of my IRA asset base. My total IRA balance at 12/31/96 was $463,843. On 12/31/2007, I have withdrawn $231,195 from my IRA. During the first 10 years my withdrawals averaged $20,000 yearly. For the 11th year, 2006, I took my minimum distribution of $31,195. On December 31, 2007, the stock fund that was invested in basic industry stocks was valued at $681,843. The international mutual fund which had all dividends reinvested and one $20,000 withdrawal transferred into the basic stock fund on April 24, 2006, was valued at $147, 861. Total value of my IRA at 12/31/2007 was $829,704.

After this eleven year study, I believed my original theory of investment positioning had been proven. Then, in August of 2008, the market was in turmoil and was extremely erratic with triple digit daily swings. I decided to wait again to see if my original investing theory was proven. As of April 2010, I believe my theory has been supported.

# IMPACT OF GOVERNMENT CHANGES

How do you decide if the dividend on the stock you are buying fits with your plan? You merely look at the 10 year Treasury bond yield published in the daily newspaper. The dividend will normally be slightly higher (about 1%) than the 10 year Treasury bond yield. If the yield on the stock is a lot more than the 10 year bond yield, and its yield is higher than its peers in the field, the low stock price probably is a direct result of either past dividend performance, or inherent risk that you may not wish to take.

What was the 10 year Treasury bond yield in April, 1996? I asked this question of my former employer, Edward Jones, and received an answer of 6.6%. Recall that I received $408,181 as a rollover into my IRA. If you multiply $400,000 by 6.6% you will receive an answer of $26,400. This explains why I believed I could withdraw an average of $20,000 per year during my sixties, and still be able to add to my stock investments.

You may ask why the interest yield on the 10 year Treasury bond is now only in the 3.7% range while the dividend yields on many good electric utility stocks are in the 5% to 6% range. First, the Federal Reserve Board has dropped the interest rates on short term borrowing for member banks several times in the past few months to prevent the country from falling deeper into recession. In the early 2000's the Federal Reserve Board lowered the interest rates 17 straight times to prevent the nation from falling into a recession. When these short term interest rates are lowered, the certificate of deposit rates are lowered, and this in turn, lowers returns that the average CD owners can obtain. This is the time that you will be extremely happy that you have invested in dividend-paying stocks.

The second reason why the dividend rates on electric utility stocks have diminished from 6.6% in April, 1996, to the present 5- 6% range has occurred from three investment changing episodes. First, Congress passed and the president signed into law an income tax break on dividend-paying stocks. Presently, this tax break is set to expire at the end of 2010 unless extended or made permanent. As of now, dividends on qualifying stocks are taxed at a maximum 15% tax rate. This law makes dividend-paying stocks more attractive to high income taxpayers. With demand for these stocks increasing, the prices have followed suit. Secondly, The Energy Policy Act of 2005 abolished depression-era geographic constraints that limited energy utilities to local markets. This law allows utilities to cross previously restricted geographic areas, and provides a climate for consolidation in the industry. The third reason is that in times of financial crisis many investors are driven to Treasury bonds for safety and protection of their assets. This demand for government security drives the prices up on Treasury bonds, causing the yields to fall.

What will happen if the maximum 15% tax rate on dividends is allowed to expire at the end of 2010? This episode alone may not cause many high yielding stocks to fall in price any lower than they are presently trading. The reason is that the stock market has probably factored in this event. In October, 2008, a few days before the presidential election, three of my utility stocks were trading with yields of over 5%, seven were trading with yields of over 6%, two weak utilities were trading with yields of over 9%, and one telephone utility was trading with a yield of over 7%. These yields were as good as or better than when I retired in 1996. 1996 was prior to the maximum 15% tax rate change on dividends and long term capital gains being adopted.

While discussing the impact of changes coming from our government, one event remembered quite well occurred in the early 1980's. Commercial real estate prices were climbing higher and higher, and commercial real estate projects were in vogue. A great deal of money had been made on real estate price increases in the late 1970's while inflationary pressures were hitting the country. Then, in the early 1980's, our government changed a law in the Internal Revenue Code. This law dealt with losses that could be used to offset taxable income on a person's income tax return. The change in law was that passive losses could only be used to offset passive income.

Passive was defined as losses on assets that were held as investments when one had no active role in managing the asset. Investors had been buying depreciable assets (like office buildings), leveraging them heavily by borrowing, depreciating them heavily, and receiving cash rents while showing large losses through depreciation. After holding the property for more than a year, the investor could sell the depreciated asset and report a capital gain taxed at the lower capital gain tax rate. When these options to save taxes could no longer be used by investors, commercial real estate fell dramatically in price. Many large commercial buildings sat empty waiting to be rented. The building of commercial property had outstripped the economic value while still being built for income tax savings. The market had to adjust and absorb the over-building of commercial property.

We have discussed a few of the past changes from the government but what does our future hold? I presently wonder about how electric utility stocks could be affected by the future. Utilities generate power from coal, wind, natural gas, solar and nuclear. The push is to create a cleaner atmosphere and shift our independence from foreign oil. One or a combination of the above sources will be needed to shift the present power source. There are impediments as well as advantages in each possibility. Wind seems a natural in windy areas but the expensive grid work for delivering the power may be prohibitive. Nuclear production has been presented as cheaper and cleaner, but after the 3 Mile Island catastrophe many years ago the "red tape" required to obtain approval for licensing takes years. In addition, most people don't want a nuclear plant in their backyards. A utility company in California is experimenting with solar panels placed on roofs of rented buildings for commercial production of electricity. This allows the utility to deliver electricity to grids already in existence. T. Boone Pickens is fighting for a mixture of wind and natural gas which he says is in bountiful supply in the United States. Although coal is the dirtiest of the choices, it is in plentiful supply. For many years utilities have had to install scrubbers in their coal plants to help with pollution. My thinking is that even though curtailment or elimination of coal as a fuel would help the atmosphere the most, there are too many jobs at stake for Congress to severely curtail its use. Whichever of the power sources become the preferred, be vigilant as to the impact it will have on your individual utility stocks. Imagine the power companies possibly becoming growth stocks because of vehicles being switched from gas engines to electric.

These examples are noted for the investor. Be aware that what may be seen as a small change in law can materially affect an investment.

# A LOOK AT THE ECONOMY IN THE YEAR 2008

People closing in on retirement, I believe, want two things. First, they want to withdraw cash from their investments so they can enjoy the fruits of their labor. Second, although they may not realize it at the time, they need to combat inflation. To do this, there needs to be some growth in their portfolios.

Presently the government is telling us that inflation is running about 3% a year. For the life of me, I don't understand how inflation is only 3%. Since I have retired in 1996, I have seen housing costs rise from $60 per square foot to $100 or more per square foot. Prescription medicine prices are out of control. Many grocery items have risen in price or reduced their product weight to keep the same price. The new worry this year is the cost of oil and how it translates to the gas for your car. If history repeats itself as I believe it does, economics will adapt. If oil continues to rise, innovations will occur. During the transition the auto companies will suffer. If commodities such as steel and lumber continue to rise, there will be a saturation point where demand will stop. When the demand slows or starts to cycle down the pain will be felt in the building industry, if not nationally, then in pockets of the country.

Ideally, a retiree should grow his investments in his IRA while being able to withdraw cash accrued from dividends. The goal must be attainable; and again, what is the secret to choosing a realistic goal? What is the benchmark?

Use the 10 year Treasury bond interest yield to guide you. In 1996, when I retired, it was hovering over 6%. It is presently hovering around 4%. The secret is to buy stocks so that the average yield will be more than the yield of the ten year government security. Presently, a good electric utility company stock has a dividend of over 5%. You can buy gas utility stocks with over a 4% dividend. Why would an individual buy a ten year Treasury bond with an interest rate of 4% when he could get 1% more immediate dividend with some growth potential? The conservative person's immediate response is, "I want the security of a government obligation." How secure is that investment if we have even the 3% yearly inflation that the government tries to maintain? After ten years you will receive your money back, but how much will that money be worth in purchasing power? You say you can sell the 10 year bond if interest begins rising, as I am fairly sure it will. You have to remember that the bond's price will adjust to the current interest rate. If interest on the 10 year bond is higher 1 year from now, your principal or bond value will be down if you want to sell it in the market. If you are having a difficult time understanding this statement, think of it this way. If a year from now, a newly issued 10 year Treasury bond has an interest rate of 5%, why would anyone pay you full price for a 10 year bond with 9 years left on the maturity and an interest rate of 4%, a full 1% below the current market? Just because you have a government security with a fixed interest rate you have not protected yourself against inflation. To protect yourself from inflation over the long run, buy a good dividend-paying stock that may increase the dividend over a 10 year period. Realize that when you buy this stock, the share price of the stock will fluctuate. If interest starts up, not unlike the 10 year Treasury bond, the price per share will go down. The difference is that if you have purchased a good company, the company will raise the dividend a few cents a year and over a 10 year period, the income on that stock will be at a considerably higher percent based on your purchase price 10 years earlier. Guess what? You don't have to worry about what the interest rate is doing 10 years from now when that 10 year Treasury bond matures.

Another conservative argument is to only buy short term certificates of deposit with 1 year or shorter maturities or government bills. In today's CD market, your living standard would deteriorate substantially unless you wanted to move in with your kids.

Apply the "Rule of 72" when buying your stock. Since the next section is devoted entirely to this rule, I will not explain it here. However, it should be thoroughly understood and committed to memory since you will use it each time you make an investment. A good dividend-paying stock in a market cycling down will be more tolerable for you.

The market will go down. Learn to appreciate the down markets. In a year or two you will have accumulated money in your cash account of your IRA that you have not needed to withdraw for living expenses and income for which you have not had to pay income taxes. You may want to purchase a new stock or add to shares you already own. Maybe when you originally purchased a stock it was yielding 4%. In recent years its dividend was raised 1 cent per quarter or 4 cents per year. Now, because of a price decrease, the stock yields 6% at the present price. Do not be afraid to buy additional shares if your holdings are well diversified. There was a saying at Edward Jones when I was there, "Buy your snow shovels in the summertime." You will be glad you did in a few years. In the meantime, you have increased your monthly income without working.

# THE RULE OF 72

The Rule of 72 is such a simple tool to use when deciding to lock in an interest rate, you would think that most people would know about it. My experience has been just the opposite. My guess is that sometime it was mentioned in a math or business class, but not studied or examined.

Anyone who wants to take some responsibility in his or her investments should learn the simple tool and use it in their decision making, whether doing their own investing, or having a professional help with their investments.

The rule is to take the interest rate or dividend you are receiving on your investment and divide it into 72. The answer you obtain is the number of years it will take for your investment to double if you reinvest all the dividends and your original investment maintains the same value. As an example, if you can get 6% on your investment, it would take 12 years for your investment to double if you reinvested all your dividends (72 divided by 6% equals 12).

It should be stated that I am not advocating reinvestment of your dividends. What I am stating is that if you can receive a 4 or 5 percent dividend from a good stock, the stock would only have to rise 1 to 2 percent yearly for your total portfolio to double in 12 years. If one were to invest in income-producing stocks paying dividends of at least 4 percent 12 years before reaching the age of 70 ½, the stock would only have to average a 2% increase each year for your investment to be worth double when you had to begin taking withdrawals from your IRA at age 70 ½ . Sure, the stock will fluctuate during this 12 year holding period. There are times when the price may be under what you gave, but as long as the stock keeps its dividend or raises the dividend over the 12 years, your objective has been attained.

Do not be overly concerned if your stock retreats in price during your holding period. Continue to focus on your objective of income being paid to your tax free IRA account. If your stock has not been damaged by some unexpected event, your company management will attempt to keep their stock dividends in the range of the dividends being paid by other stocks in their category.

Do not be swayed by those people who seek fixed rates. Their idea of safety is misleading. Using the Rule of 72, how safe do you think these people felt when the Federal Reserve Board continued to drop interest for a total of 17 times in the early 2000's until certificates of deposit were paying just 2% yearly? It would have taken 36 years for that investment to double if they had been able to reinvest all the interest without taking distributions. In the meantime, the Federal Reserve Board prides itself on having done a good job if they keep inflationary pressure at 3% or less. If you are living on your retirement income from your IRA under that scenario, you may want to seek ways of reducing your life span to match the end of your money.

This may prove a little drastic!

# SETTING A GOAL

Setting goals is one of the most important features of your investment planning. Keep in mind that your goal will change during your years of investing. During the early stages of your working years you should probably try to obtain more growth in your investment portfolio. During your later years, you should probably strive to obtain growth but be more conservative.

During your sixties, your goal should begin to change. Let's call it the 10 year plan. Under the present law, at 70½ you must take minimum distributions from your retirement plan. Prior to 70½ you may want to take distributions from your plan to satisfy your lifestyle.

My reason for writing this guide is to help the retiree be able to withdraw funds from his IRA without selling his investments. To accomplish this goal, you will be required to buy individual stocks that pay good dividends and have those dividends deposited to your IRA for withdrawal or additional investing. During your fifties or sixties, before your minimum distribution is required, you need to set a reachable goal.

Within the following pages, I will give you parameters to follow as well as important hints to use for setting a reasonable goal.

If you don't have a goal, you cannot judge how your plan is proceeding. Once you set a reachable goal, try not to change the objective. There are times when stock market swings may tempt you to withdraw from the stock market. This could be very disruptive to your goal. Think long and hard before taking this action. My hope is that after reading this guide, you will have the confidence to trust the goal you have set and stay the course.

Once the goal is set, the investor may want help in its implementation. There is nothing wrong with seeking professional help, but the investor has to be responsible for the investments made. The reasons are numerous but the bottom line is that one tends to pay more attention when their financial well-being is at stake. Relay your guidelines to your advisor to follow, and make sure before making any purchases that your advisor is adhering to the guidelines.

As any investor will attest, with all available information, there will be some mistakes made. The secret is to keep your batting averages as high as possible. Diversify your purchases by company. If one company does not satisfy your parameters, get rid of the investment. You haven't bailed on your entire portfolio, only a small percentage.

Write your goal at the front of your plan. My goal was to have dividends paid into my IRA cash account so that when I reached 70½ and was required to withdraw a minimum distribution, I could withdraw those distributions from cash without selling investments to meet the requirement. During my 60's, I had a set amount that I could withdraw yearly while still adding to my stock investments.

By reaching your goal, you can add to the shares of stock you own. Each additional share of stock will add cash to your plan. If at the end of a plan year, the market value of your total fund is down like it was at the end of 2009, your minimum distribution required will be lower, but this will allow you to take a larger distribution than the minimum requirement or use the extra cash to purchase additional shares of stock to help increase your cash balance for distribution the following year.

By adding to your stock numbers yearly, upon your death you should be able to pass a nice portfolio of stocks to your spouse, and eventually, to the next generation while still satisfying your lifestyle during retirement.

# CONFIDENCE

Confidence in yourself is probably the most important consideration when contemplating your retirement. Stock is the one purchase that the mainstream public hesitates to buy when it's on sale. This phenomenon occurs because every minute of every day the fluctuating price of the stock is listed. Human nature takes over. One can judge if they paid a good or a bad purchase price. If the price of the stock retreats from what they paid, they feel they made a bad purchase. If for no other reason, this is why one should judge a stock's worth not by its listed value, but by the dividend that will be received.

Compare stock with land. Land is purchased for what it will return. You can grow crops for a profit; you can feed cattle for a profit; you can rent for a profit. You don't think about losses and you don't see the land priced after you purchase it.

This illustration was brought home to me once when working as a stockbroker. I had a potential client come to my office after I had pitched him a SEP-IRA (Simplified Employee Pension) plan. A SEP was ideal for him because he was the only person working his farm. His first comment was he had never purchased stock because of the risk involved. I said, "Wait a minute. You have thousands of dollars invested in farming equipment. If you had to sell it tomorrow, you would only receive a fraction of what you paid for it. All of your farm land is rented. Your living comes from raising good crops of corn, maize and wheat. While the crops are growing, you have to depend on Mother Nature for water, sun and no hail. When you harvest your crops, the elevator gives you a price based on supply and demand for your grain. I would think about the safest asset you could have would be good stock. The additional benefits are that you get to deduct your investment when you purchase it and you don't have to pay income tax on any dividends or capital gains while it is growing for you. Your biggest concern will be paying income tax when you begin your withdrawals after you retire." I told him to go home and think about the pros and cons of having a retirement plan. He came back the following day. As our relationship grew, money came out of the woodwork. Upon retirement, he had tax-free bonds, tax-free mutual funds and a substantial balance in his SEP-IRA. I will never forget the day when I told him he had become a millionaire. He mentioned it most days he came to the office. He and I both had a great feeling of accomplishment.

The guidelines highlighted in this study will help you build your confidence.

During your working years, hopefully you invested in your employers' 401(k) or 403(b) plan and possibly, you have an IRA. Most of these plans invest in stock and bond mutual funds. It is now time to think about investing on your own. For the time being you may want to continue with your mutual fund investments. But, if your plan allows you to buy individual stocks, think about putting a small part into an individual stock. Do not look for a high growth stock. Do that through your mutual funds. Buy a stock that pays a good dividend relative to the rest of the market. My suggestion is to buy a good electric utility to help gain that confidence. As I have stated before, utilities are mostly income type stocks with some growth potential over a period of years.

Remember the "Rule of 72" featured in a previous chapter of this guide. Look for a stock that has raised its dividend a penny or two over the past year.

It would be even better if the utility has a history of raising the dividend a few cents yearly over a number of years. A stockbroker should be able to help you with this hunt. An analysis from a Standard and Poor's Investment service could be helpful, or you can find the information on the internet if you are computer savvy. When choosing your stock make sure the earnings per share adequately cover the dividend. You will find that utility stocks pay out a lot higher percent of their per share earnings than most companies. Also, because of the nature of a utility, they have a large part of their balance sheet in fixed assets and a large part of their liabilities as long term debt. Do not concentrate on assets and liabilities in the balance sheet. Make sure the dividends paid to their shareholders are covered by the earnings and that they have a tendency to raise their dividends yearly. The more popular utilities will have a lower dividend per share than their peers. When deciding on a utility stock, buy one that has a dividend of at least 1% to 2% higher than the current 10 year Treasury bond interest yield. If the dividend is higher than the utility peers, it probably means it has more risk involved. It may not raise its dividends yearly, or it may be in a cash-strapped situation that will cause it to lower the dividend at a later date.

Note that we are using two of our basic concepts. We are applying the Rule of 72 and monitoring the current yield of the ten year Treasury bond.

# DON'T COUNT YOUR CHICKENS BEFORE THEY HATCH

"Don't count your chickens before they hatch," OR "Do not calculate the quantity of juvenile poultry before the proper period of incubation has fully materialized." (I have to admit I sometimes use this latter phrase with my grandchildren to watch their reactions.)

I use the two phrases here to make two points. First, keep your investments simple. Second, invest in companies that already have earnings and pay dividends. Ask yourself: What does everyone need in their everyday life? Everyone needs utilities for their homes. Everyone needs gas and oil for their cars and trucks. Everyone in this day and age seems to need a cell phone. Everyone needs food; however, investing in food stocks can be tricky because of private labels competing with branded products that have been around for years. The best part of this simplicity is that companies producing these products are among the group paying the higher dividends. Dividends should be part of your plan to build cash for distribution or to diversify your stock portfolio if you are not ready for a withdrawal from your plan. Once you decide upon a company stock for purchase, study their dividend history. Look for companies that have a history of increasing dividends yearly. A few cents per share added yearly will help you keep up with inflation.

The second point I want to stress is transparency. Buying individual companies gives you more information about that particular investment. If you are not comfortable in making your own investment decisions, seek the advice of a professional. But, make sure the professional understands your goal of buying companies that pay and raise their dividends yearly. Once you buy a company's stocks, should you have the dividend reinvested to purchase more of the company stock? That is a personal choice. I chose not to reinvest the dividends. This allows you to build cash for diversification or withdrawal. I wanted my IRA to receive the cash for simplicity and transparency. You know your stock basis (the purchase price of the stock) and you do not have to constantly adjust the stock basis each time you receive a dividend. You know that your basis will remain static and you are able to judge the stock performance against its stock category.

We cannot leave this chapter without discussing mutual funds, ETF's and hedge funds. During your working years, mutual funds are a good choice for investment. By investing the dividends through good and bad markets, your investment will grow over time.

Mutual funds have transparency. I used a mix of growth, conservative growth, and foreign companies. Tell your investment advisor what you are interested in accomplishing. Mutual fund companies have designed their funds to accomplish the desired purpose. Your main concern should be that the mutual fund company has a good investment record when compared with their peers. Make sure you take into account the annual fees provided in their prospectus when comparing funds. I used funds with less than 0.7% annual fees. If your plan allows it, as you get within four or five years of retirement you may want to begin investing in individual dividend-paying stocks with part of your yearly contribution. Upon retirement, I recommend keeping your foreign stock mutual funds when you roll your investments into an IRA. In my personal IRA, I began with about ten percent in a dividend-paying foreign stock mutual fund.

I reinvested all of the dividends and set a goal for it not to grow to over twenty percent of my total IRA. You accomplish this by cashing some of the mutual fund after it has had a good profitable year-end using the cash to buy additional dividend-paying stocks within your IRA.

ETF stands for Exchange-Traded Funds. They are like mutual funds in that they have a group of stocks in them targeted for a specific purpose. ETF's began trading sometime around 2005. Their numbers and types have grown substantially since their introduction and presently there are over seven hundred of them. ETF's can be bought and sold while the market is open at their listed prices like an individual stock. The price of an ETF is primarily determined by the net asset value of the stocks which it holds. However, the price may be impacted by the supply or demand of particular stocks in the portfolio. Even though the stocks in the fund are shown, I believe the individual investor should be aware of the complexity of valuation. Because of the short timeframe that ETF's have been in existence, their track record may be difficult to determine. If one wants to gamble with a small part of his or her portfolio, ETF's may give the desired result.

I do not recommend hedge funds except for the very wealthy. The minimum investment in hedge funds is at least $200,000 with a much larger net worth. There is no transparency and at this time, the Securities and Exchange Commission (SEC) seems to have no desire to regulate them. Because of this lack of transparency, several large investor frauds surfaced when the stock market tanked in 2008 and 2009.

# BASIC INDUSTRY STOCKS
# VERSUS BONDS

Many if not all financial planners would not consider my portfolio of stocks to be diversified. I have the explanation. When I retired in April, 1996, I was concerned, just as I am today, about inflation devouring purchasing power. By using the Rule of 72 and applying a 3% yearly inflation rate, the fund would be worth half as much in purchasing power in 24 years time as it was in 1996. The rule of thumb in 1996 was that as a person grew older, more and more of his funds should be in "safe" secured bonds. The problem with that theory is that even though you may receive your principal when the bond matures, the cash won't be worth as much. I thought then and I think now, that you should try to get some principal growth. An additional problem, when investing in bonds, is that you have to buy long-term maturities to receive a decent yield.  Again, the rule of thumb in 1996 was that a 70-year-old person should have 70% of the fund in fixed interest.  I chose what I consider a safer approach.  I am 73 years old.  Seventy three percent of my funds are in basic industry stocks.  Fifty nine percent of my funds are in utility stocks.  I consider these gas and electric utilities to be as safe as long term bonds and they provide some growth potential.  My utility stocks have had a good record of raising dividends a few cents per share annually.

As a side note, many companies who issue lower rated bonds will acquire a AAA-rating by insuring the bonds against default.  Because of this AAA-rating, the issuer is able to pay a lower interest rate.  In 2008 and 2009, insurance companies that insure these bonds were found to have inadequate capital to return capital to the investor if the bond defaulted.  This caused many AAA-rated bonds to lose their rating and suddenly become less valuable with the prices falling accordingly.

My biggest concern with investing in bonds is inflation. If and when inflation occurs, new bonds coming to market will have to sell with a higher rate of interest to gain acceptance. The older bonds in the market will drop in value to align themselves with the interest rate of the new bonds. What this means to the investor is that to recoup his principal, he will have to wait until maturity which may be many years away.

To further explain my personal stock fund investments, most individual stocks represent 5% or less of the total fund. The personal stock fund (Exhibit II) reflects 22 stocks that represent 84.57% of the total fund. The international world fund that holds many foreign stocks represents 14.63% of the total fund. The few dollars left are in cash.

# CORRELATION BETWEEN THE DOW UTILITY INDEX AND THE 10 YEAR TREASURY BOND

Sometime during my early years as a broker for Edward Jones I was told that utility stocks are the first to decline in a falling stock market and the first stocks to rise in an advancing market. This simple statement came in useful during my years as a broker, but I always wondered what exactly caused this phenomenon to occur. As I studied this process over the years, I discovered, I believe, a reason.

Before discussing the reason, allow me to explain the Dow Jones Stock Indexes. The total Dow Jones Index consists of 65 stocks. There are three categories: The Dow Jones Industrial Average consists of 30 companies, the Dow Jones Transportation Average consists of 20 companies, and the Dow

Jones Utilities Average consists of 15 companies. These three sections comprise the Dow Jones Index. When you see a reference to the Dow Jones Averages in the newspaper, it is normally referring to only the Dow Jones Industrial Average.

There seems to be a definite correlation between the Dow Jones Utility Index and the price and interest yield of the 10 year Treasury bond. As people become skeptical of the market's advance, they begin buying more conservative stocks such as utilities. When skepticism turns to pessimism, people turn to even safer purchases such as U.S. Treasury bonds. When they sell utility stocks to buy 10 year Treasury bonds, the utility stocks drop in price and the 10 year bond price advances. The advance in the bond price drops the interest yield and at some point in time, buyers begin buying utility stocks again once the price has declined enough that the dividends paid on the stock result in a significantly better yield than the 10 year Treasury bond. (The price and interest yield on bonds is discussed in detail within the chapter, "Basic Industry Stocks Versus Bonds.")

This simple hint allows an investor to better decide when to purchase a stock. Watch the Dow Jones Utility Index shown in the daily newspaper and compare the movement with the 10 year Treasury bond yield and the Dow Jones Industrial Index. There will be times when the Utility Index is up while the Industrial Index is still going down. If this occurs, note what the 10 year bond yield is doing. If the interest yield is higher than the prior day, people have begun to sell the bond. (This drives the price down and the interest yield higher.) If the 10 year Treasury bond yield has risen and the Dow Jones Utility Index has risen, you may have a buying opportunity for utility stocks even when the Dow Jones Industrial Index is still headed lower. Remember that a good utility stock should have at least a 1-2% better dividend yield than the interest yield on the 10 year Treasury bond. If your newspaper does not show both the Dow Jones Industrial Index and the Dow Jones Utility Index, you can obtain the indexes from a TV channel or the internet.

# WHEN TO SELL A STOCK

This guide's purpose is to buy stocks and hold them for the dividends. However when to sell a stock is a decision as important as when to buy. During my 14-plus years of study and analysis during my retirement, I have decided upon certain criteria. When I strayed from the criteria, the consequences proved painful.

**Rule #1** – If a company cuts the dividend it pays, sell the stock unless the dividend yield compares favorably to other stocks in its sector.

**Rule #2** – If a company has a major catastrophe, sell the stock. If the news media begins naming names, you will be better off without the risk of a falling stock price.

**Rule #3** – If an electric utility is only paying a 3% dividend or less based on its price, sell the stock. The price is too high for the dividend to support. A caveat to this sale is another company may have made an offer to buy the company you own. This action may cause the price to shoot up close to the offer price. There are times when the price per share will even go higher than the offer price. This indicates that some investors believe there will be competing bids or a higher offer. At this point you will have to decide what is in your best interest. There are too many scenarios possible for you to make a decision without more facts. Keep in mind, though, that an offer can be withdrawn or your company management may turn down the offer. If this happens, the stock price will fall to where it was trading before the offer.

**Rule #4** – If there is a buy-out of your company and the offer is for cash plus stock in the purchasing company, I found it safer to sell the stock that was issued by the purchaser. There are too many unknown facts on how the purchaser intends to finance the purchase.

**Rule #5** – There are times when the entire sector or category of the stock you hold may be in stress. (This happened with the financial sector during 2008 and 2009.) In that situation, all of the companies in the sector may reduce their dividends and your company's dividend still compares favorably with the sector. When the whole sector is in turmoil, it's probably better to sell your stock and replace it at a later date when there is more transparency as to how your particular company will succeed.

**Rule #6** – There are times when a company you own may spin-off some of its assets and liabilities to form another company. At this point, you will own shares in the new company. If this happens, you will need to determine if the spin-off fits within your objective and goal. I found that if only a few shares of the new company were issued for my holdings in the original company, it was best to sell the new, spin-off shares.

# ANALYSIS OF EXHIBITS

## Comparison of IRA at 12/31/07 (Exhibit I) and IRA at 3/26/10 (Exhibit II) along with history of cash withdrawals and account balances (Exhibit III)

Exhibit III reflects that over the 14 year period, cash withdrawals were $292,624. The stock account balance was $423,110 in 1996 and is valued at $571,844 at March 26, 2010. The Capital World Mutual Fund was $40,733 at 12/31/96, has had two withdrawals (transferred to the stock fund) of $45,000, has had all dividends reinvested, and is valued at $97,958 at March 26, 2010. (March 26, 2010, was used for the 14 year totals because the Edward Jones month-end statement was valued at that date.) The total fund was valued at $463,843 on 12/31/96. After

14 years of withdrawals totaling $292,624, the total fund is valued at $669,802 as of March 26, 2010. This balance compares favorably with the account balances during the fourteen years shown except for the inflated 2006 and 2007 total account balances.

More in-depth analysis shows that at December 31, 2007, the stock fund was valued at $681,843. The stock fund value is decreased by $73,571 or 11.4% after the $25,000 addition made in January 2008 from the mutual fund and two withdrawals totaling $61,425 made in 2008 and 2010 (a net withdrawal of $36,425).

The mutual fund balance was $147,861 at 12/31/07. The mutual fund balance is $97,958 at 3/26/10. After adjusting for the $25,000 withdrawal made in January 2008, the balance decreased $24,903 or 20.27% from the 12/31/07 balance. Meanwhile, the Standard and Poor's 500 Stock Index is up 79% from a 12 year low in March 2009. However, it is still down 23% from its October 2007, high of 1,565.

At March 26, 2010, the Capital World mutual fund represents 14.63% (Exhibit II) of the total fund as compared to 17.82% (Exhibit I) of the total on December 31, 2007. During this time period, the personal stock fund has performed better than the Capital World mutual fund.

## Exhibit I Dividends 2007 compared to Exhibit II Dividends 2010

Yearly dividends projected at December 31, 2007, were $28,503 compared to projected yearly dividends for 2010 of $28,908. Since a cash withdrawal was not required during 2009, the cash was used to add one utility stock, one oil and gas stock, and one telephone company stock. All three of these stocks were what I considered basic industry stocks. From December

31, 2007, to March 26, 2010, 14 of 19 basic industry stocks raised dividends; 2 raised dividends 3 times, 10 raised dividends twice, 2 raised dividends once, 1 raised the dividend in December 2007, 2 were new purchases and 2 stocks had dividends lowered. The two utilities stocks where dividends were lowered were not sold because the dividend yield still compared favorably with other stocks in their category.

Not shown by the exhibits but a noteworthy point is that on April 6, 2010 (only 6 actual trading days between March 26 and April 6 because of Good Friday and two weekends) the 14 utility stocks had a value of $408,582 as compared to a value of $395,875 at 3/26/10 (Exhibit II), an increase of $12,707, or 3.21%. On Monday, April 5, the 10-year Treasury bond yield climbed above 4% for the first time since June 2009. The 10-year Treasury bond traded up on April 6, along with the utilities, causing the yield to fall to 3.96%. This 4% yield on the 10-year Treasury bond has not remained at the 4% level since October 2008. This is noteworthy because utility stocks are defensive stocks. They are often bought when there is market concern about stocks being overpriced. The demand for the utility stocks drives the price up. It appears that after the large rise in utility stocks on April 6, traders became even more hesitant and shifted to 10-year Treasuries, thus lowering the yield below the 4% level.

No one can predict the stock market, but allow me to make some observations: The stock market was on sale beginning in March 2009, and continuing during 2009. Four to six percent dividend yields were available on high quality stocks during that period. Presently, the market is still advancing, but the volumes of daily stocks traded have reduced considerably. The government has borrowed a lot of money by issuing bonds. This money was then used to bail out financial institutions and auto manufacturers, to increase the length of time people can receive unemployment, to provide incentives to help people buy homes and cars...the list goes on. While doing this, the government has managed to keep the interest rates artificially low. They have reduced the Federal Reserve rate of interest about as low as they can. They have managed to do this because inflation has not become unmanageable. The heavy borrowing and the incentives have to stop or the U.S. government debt rating will be jeopardized. That would not be a pretty picture. Inflation would return with a vengeance and interest rates would rise sharply.

In addition, today is April 15, 2010; the last day one can receive a 2009 income tax deduction by funding their IRA. Mutual funds will receive more cash than usual. These cash funds will be available for mutual funds to invest. If the cash is invested in stocks, the volume and prices will go higher. However, if the mutual fund managers are concerned about the stock market, increases to cash received will be invested in short term debt instruments such as government bills, notes or bonds.

The reader is probably aware of these observations. I reiterate them to make a point. If one has available cash in his IRA or other retirement account, as of this writing (April 15, 2010), I believe over the next several months the stock market will recede enabling you to avail yourself of dividend yields seen during 2009.

**EXHIBIT I**

**INDIVIDUAL RETIREMENT ACCOUNT BALANCES**

**AT DECEMBER 31, 2007**

| No. of Co. | SHARES | COST BASIS | MARKET VALUE | 2007 YEARLY DIVIDENDS | DIVIDEND PERCENTAGE AT COST | AT MARKET | PERCENT OF TOTAL ASSET BASE |
|---|---|---|---|---|---|---|---|
| 13 | 14,795-GAS & ELECTRIC UTITLIES | $350,530 | $ 469,772 | $ 19,740 | 5.63% | 4.20% | 56.62% |
| 1 | 1,000- TELEPHONE UTILITY | 23,999 | 41,560 | 1,420 | 5.92% | 3.42% | 5.01% |
| 2 | 680-GAS AND OIL COMPANIES | 20,867 | 62,056 | 1,363 | 6.53% | 2.20% | 7.48% |
| | BASIC INDUSTRY STOCKS | $395,396 | $573,388 | $22,523 | 5.70% | 3.93% | 69.11% |
| 1 | 1,000-CONVERTIBLE PREFERRED AUTO | 52,025 | 32,450 | 3,250 | 6.25% | 10.02% | 3.91% |
| 1 | 300-INDUSTRIALS | 9,421 | 11,121 | 336 | 3.57% | 3.02% | 1.34% |
| 2 | 1,400-FINANCIAL SERVICES | 52,644 | 22,990 | (H) 2,249 | Not Applicable | | 2.77% |
| 1 | 500 HEALTHCARE | 12,362 | 11,365 | (Q) 145 | Not Applicable | | 1.37% |
| 2 | 700 SPIN-OFFS FROM STOCK HELD | 2,542 | 1,043 | 0 | | | 0.13% |
| | | $524,390 | $652,357 | $28,503 | | | 78.63% |
| | ADD CASH HELD | | 29,486 | | | | 3.55% |
| | TOTAL VALUE OF STOCK FUND | | $681,843 | | | | 82.18% |
| | MUTUAL FUND:INTERNATIONAL | | 147,861 | | | | 17.82% |
| | TOTAL MARKET VALUE OF I.R.A@12-31-07 | | $829,704 | | | | 100.00% |

(H) – HALF A YEAR

(Q) – QUARTER OF A YEAR

EXHIBIT II

INDIVIDUAL RETIREMENT ACCOUNT BALANCES

AT MARCH 26, 2010

| No. of Co. | SHARES | COST BASIS | 3/26/2010 MARKET VALUE | 2010 YEARLY DIVIDENDS | DIVIDEND PERCENTAGE AT COST | DIVIDEND PERCENTAGE AT MARKET | PERCENT OF TOTAL ASSET BASE |
|---|---|---|---|---|---|---|---|
| 14 | 15,015 - GAS & ELECTRIC UTITIES | $358,643 | $395,875 | $19,882 | 5.54% | 5.02% | 59.10% |
| 2 | 1,400- TELEPHONE UTILITIES | $35,973 | $38,388 | $2,440 | 6.78% | 6.36% | 5.73% |
| 3 | 880-GAS AND OIL COMPANIES | $28,899 | $55,396 | $2,376 | 8.22% | 4.29% | 8.27% |
| | BASIC INDUSTRY STOCKS | $423,515 | $489,659 | $24,698 | 5.83% | 5.04% | 73.10% |
| 1* | 1,000-CONVERTIBLE PREFERRED AUTO | $52,025 | $48,720 | $3,250 | 6.25% | 6.67% | 7.27% |
| 1 | 600-INDUSTRIALS | $15,137 | $11,004 | $240 | 1.59% | 2.18% | 1.64% |
| 2** | 1,400-FINANCIAL SERVICES | $0 | $0 | $0 | | | 0.00% |
| 1 | 1,000 HEALTHCARE | $24,038 | $17,140 | $720 | 3.00% | 4.20% | 2.56% |
| 1 | 200 SPIN-OFFS FROM STOCK HELD | $2,541 | $197 | $0 | | | 0.03% |
| | | $517,256 | $566,720 | $28,908 | | | 11.50% |
| | ADD: CASH | | $5,124 | | | | 0.77% |
| | TOTAL VALUE OF STOCK FUND | | $571,844 | | | | |
| | MUTUAL FUND:INTERNATIONAL | | $97,958 | | | | 14.63% |
| | TOTAL MARKET VALUE OF I.R.A.@3-26-10 | | $669,802 | | | | 100.00% |

*Note #1 on next page

**Note #2 on next page

## Notes to Exhibit II – Individual Retirement Account Balances Ending March 26, 2010

**\*Note #1** - One thousand shares of auto convertible preferred is callable by the company. If called, the stock would be called in at $50 per share. The stock was issued at $50 per share in early 2002 with a 6.5% dividend yield. Since purchasing the stock, I have received cash dividends of $22,554.58. The last quarterly dividend of $812.50 was received January 15, 2009. Presently there have been 4 quarters at $812.50 per quarter or $3,250 of dividends unpaid. The company has the right to accrue these dividends, but it is my understanding that past dividends have to be paid within five years of deferment or paid if the stock is called. The stock can be converted to 2.83 shares of the company's common stock and therefore tracks at the price of the common stock. You will notice the stock has increased $16,270 since the December 31, 2007, price shown in exhibit I.

**\*\*Note #2** - The December 31, 2007 account balances show 2 financial services stocks with a cost of $52,644 and a market value of $22,990. One of these had a cost of $11,983.80 and a market value of $9,380 on December 31, 2007. On January 29, 2008, I added 600 shares at an additional cost of $15,598.67 for a total cost of $27,582.47. On January 21, 2010, I sold the entire 1,000 shares for $7378.42. My total loss was $20,204.05. Based on the December 31, 2007, market value of 400 shares plus the 600 additional shares purchased after December 31, 2007, the loss was $17,600.25.

On December 31, 2007, I held 1,000 shares of the other financial services stock purchased between November 2004, and July 2007. My total cost in the stock on December 31, 2007, was $40,659.87 with a market value of $13,610. This was a stock that blindsided me completely. From the first dividend I received on February 15, 2005, through August 15, 2007, the company had raised the dividend $0.01 per share quarterly, or $0.04 per year. The dividend was not raised in November 2007, but I still received $560 for the quarter. The dividend was reduced to $0.15 per share on 2/15/08 and slashed again on 5/15/08. In April 2008, I sold 500 shares, half the shares I owned, at $5,724.18. This resulted in a loss of $14,161.43. I kept 500 shares that had cost $20,774.26, and basically rode the shares to zero, getting a net of $31.99 for them, a loss of $20,742.27. This one bad stock resulted in a total loss of $34,903.70 of my cost. Based on the market value on 12/31/07, I suffered a loss of $7,853.83. These two financial stocks lost $25,454.08 from December 31, 2007, until sold.

EXHIBIT III
YEAR ENDING BALANCES AND CASH WITHDRAWALS BY YEAR
AT DECEMBER 31 AND AT MARCH 26, 2010

| TOTALS AT YEAR END | WITHDRAWALS FROM MUTUAL FUND | YEARLY CASH WITHDRAWALS FROM STOCK ACCT. | CASH BALANCE INCLUDED IN STOCK ACCT. | BALANCE OF STOCK ACCOUNT (INCLUDING CASH) | MUTUAL FUND BALANCE: CAPITAL WORLD GROWTH & INCOME | ACCOUNT TOTAL |
|---|---|---|---|---|---|---|
| 12/31/1996 | | $0 | $67,450 | $423,110 | $40,733 | $463,843 |
| 1997 | | $24,000 | $36,196 | $507,530 | $48,051 | $555,581 |
| 1998 | | $33,895 | $24,296 | $531,498 | $55,826 | $587,324 |
| 1999 | | $15,000 | $34,021 | $441,420 | $71,057 | $512,477 |
| 2000 | | $15,000 | $54,715 | $610,198 | $72,026 | $682,224 |
| 2001 | | $24,000 | $98,105 | $581,529 | $68,454 | $649,983 |
| 2002 | | $23,000 | $6,725 | $445,242 | $63,560 | $508,802 |
| 2003 | | $21,100 | $18,657 | $528,642 | $88,393 | $617,035 |
| 2004 | | $22,000 | $15,373 | $568,394 | $105,555 | $673,949 |
| 2005 | | $12,005 | $28,698 | $562,996 | $121,092 | $684,088 |
| 4/24/06 Deposited to Stock | -$20,000 | | | $20,000 | | |
| 2006 | | $10,000 | $59,210 | $700,869 | $125,813 | $826,682 |
| 2007 | | $31,196 | $29,486 | $681,843 | $147,861 | $829,704 |
| Total Cash Draws as of 12/31/2007 | | $231,196 | | | | |
| 1/29/08 Deposited to Stock (Sold 505,034 shares) | -$25,000 | | | $25,000 | | |
| 2008 | | $32,410 | $24,915 | $503,217 | $74,484 | $577,701 |
| 2009* | | $0 | $32,927.31 | $592,118 | $98,508 | $690,627 |
| 1/29/10 Withdrawal of 2009 Minimum Distribution | | $29,018 | | | | |
| Totals at March 26, 2010 | | | $5,124 | $571,844 | $97,958 | $669,802 |
| Total Cash Draws as of March 26, 2010 | | $292,624 | | | | |

*Congress suspended the 2008 minimum distribution requirement because of stock market conditions. Therefore, no withdrawal was taken in 2009 dictated by the 2008 year end balances. The extra cash was used to increase the basic industry stocks during April 2009.

CPSIA information can be obtained at www.ICGtesting.com
Printed in the USA
BVOW021224080212

282454BV00006B/3/P